SURVIVING IN SPIRIT

A Memoir about Sisterhood and Addiction

MELANIE BERLIET

THOUGHT CATALOG BOOKS

Copyright © 2015 by The Thought & Expression Co.

All rights reserved. Published by Thought Catalog Books, a division of The Thought & Expression Co., Williamsburg, Brooklyn.

For general information and submissions: hello@thoughtcatalog.com.

First edition, 2015.

ISBN 978-1515177562

10 9 8 7 6 5 4 3 2 1

Founded in 2010, Thought Catalog is a website and imprint dedicated to your ideas and stories. We publish fiction and non-fiction from emerging and established writers across all genres.

DEDICATION

To Damien

"As brother and sister we go together, or we stop."

-Xhabbo, A Far Off Place

PRAISE FOR SURVIVING IN SPIRIT

"Mélanie's writing is honest and thought provoking, but also entertaining. Without a doubt, she keeps it interesting."—**Jared Cohen,** New York Times best-selling author of *The New Digital Age: Reshaping the Future of People, Nations, and Business* and *Children of Jihad: A Young American's Travels Among the Youth of the Middle East*

"Inspired by her sister's untimely death to buck convention and lead a full life, Mélanie's story is uniquely tragic, but relatable to anyone familiar with life's capacity to shock and the challenge of searching for self. This book will resonate with you long after you've finished it." —**Meghan McCain,** best-selling author of *America, You Sexy Bitch: A Love Letter to Freedom* and *Dirty Sexy Politics*

"You should be very excited to read about Melanie's adventures with addiction and married men since it's probably the safest way to experience both."—**Joel Stein,** TIME columnist and author of *Man Made: In Which a Dad Learns to be a Man for His Son*

"Mélanie's writing is funny, sexy, and intelligent." —**Brian Donovan,** author of the best-selling Amazon Single, *Not A Match: My True Tales of Online Dating Disasters*

AUTHOR'S NOTE

As with any reconstruction of memory, I had to estimate the timing of certain events and/or massage minor details governing certain scenarios, but without altering the content of my experience. I also changed the names and defining characteristics of a few people mentioned to protect their identities. Basically, all of this actually happened—as best I can remember it.

INTRODUCTION

As the second child, I grew up witnessing my older sister's firsts with a mix of jealousy, awe, and irritation. Céline was the first to ride her bike to school, the first to babysit, the first to squander her earnings on Hostess cupcakes behind Mom and Dad's backs, the first to travel alone, the first to drive, and the first to go away to college. It never occurred to me that my "first envy" could expire.

But throughout our twenties, as Céline's alcoholism advanced, she seemed to blossom more like a self cannibalizing Venus Flytrap than the dignified orchid I once admired. I watched as my older sister was the first to get wasted before breakfast, to go broke, to collapse in public, to steal, to enter rehab, to get an abortion, and to date a certified crackhead. Though I grew somewhat numb to Céline's shocking behavior over time, nothing could prepare me for her very last first: Dying.

By the time Céline died, she was Kermit The Frog green and she vomited blood more frequently than she was able to eat. My older sister had gone from summa cum laude Columbia graduate to NYU PhD student to unemployed, rambling, stumbling drunk who told gratuitous lies, neglected to pay rent, and collected inexplicably icky bruises.

By the time Céline died, I was no longer a Miss Goody Two Shoes from a waspy Connecticut suburb trotting down the Sensible Path. I was an adult whose career (and love life) involved testing the waters of the socially unconventional, and, at times, unacceptable.

How exactly did this happen? And how are our stories intertwined?

Before I became a writer, I was a bond trader—one secure rung on an elite investment bank's proverbial corporate ladder, happily on track to make shitloads of money like I'd always planned. By the time I was a six-figure salaried 23-year-old, however, a basic, unwelcome lesson had crept up on me: No amount of money can buy happiness, and no pair of overpriced stilettos can make this gal enjoy trading bonds. Two meltdowns and a bottle of tequila later, I quit Wall Street in pursuit of *something* else.

What leads a young woman to abandon the safe bounds of convention—to gamble a stable livelihood couched in health insurance, regular paychecks, Barney's shopping excursions and expensable Nobu dinners—for the unknown?

At first, all I understood was that I'd lost my sense of what 'supposed to' meant. And that my sister was sick.

Though I can't credit Céline's alcoholism completely for inspiring me to leave Wall Street in search of some way to make a living beyond glorified gambling and the glorious paycheck that went with it, it seems more than coincidental that her illness took root around the same time, in the early aughts.

As Céline's illness escalated, I flailed about trying to establish a career and an existence that made some kind of sense. I had no plan to speak of—only a recently realized passion for reading and writing, and a nagging sense that was foolish to agonize over what I was supposed to do/think/know/read/listen to/watch/feel, or who I was supposed to be/befriend/love/like/learn from. The harsh reality that my sister of all people had a major problem forced me to question why the fuck 'supposed to' mattered so damn much. So in my desperate search for self, I pitched projects that sounded crazy and/or dangerous to most, but which gave me a thrill and enabled me to establish a career as an immersive journalist. I grew some balls, so to speak, as I stopped giving a shit about what others might think.

Gradually, you see, another basic lesson was creeping up on me: Life is beautifully short, and fragile as fuck. Life happens. And while it's tough to understand what leads a person into addiction—to witness someone you love kind-of kill herself—the truth is that you can learn from it.

When I visited my sister at the hospital once late in her illness, she barely looked alive, saggy breasts peeking through a haphazardly tied gown. Céline had one request that day: a bottle of the spray-on dry shampoo Mom gets from relatives in France. On the brink of death, all she wanted was to clean her matted strands. This heartbreakingly simple wish wasn't about appearances; it was about comfort. Moments like this thrust perspective upon me.

Since the day I was born I have been Céline's sister, and my path—from square Wall-Streeter-with-a-grand-plan to carefree intrepid journo—is understandable only through the lens of our lovingly complicated relationship. The devastating beauty of what happened to Céline led me to question who I am and to figure things out for myself. However unwittingly, my sister empowered me to take risks, and to live.

***

The immersive method is inherently personal, and honest. It follows, then, that I would delve into my personal history to explore what guided me toward such an odd livelihood.

The details of my story may be unique, but the rite of passage they constitute is relatable. Self-discovery throughout one's twenties is at the forefront of our collective consciousness. Consider the 2011 New York Magazine feature, "The Kids Are Actually Sort of Alright," and the 2010 New York Times Magazine feature, "What Is It About 20-Somethings?" both of which went wildly viral and pointed to the fact that today's young adults flail about for longer than previous generations. Popular sitcoms such as *Two Broke Girls, How I Met Your Mother, Girls* and *New Girl* showcase characters entrenched in this period of "emerging adulthood." Maybe it's a luxury and a curse for millenials to want so much and to take so much time figuring it all out. Whatever the case, I now count myself a card-carrying grown-up with an unorthodox—and yet, ordinary—story to share.

I

On April 3rd, 2009, when Dad calls to report that Céline is unconscious, the first thing I do is devise a new calendar. As soon as my 30-year-old sister wakes up, we'll start referring to years as either BCLC (Before Céline Lost Consciousness) or ACLC (After Céline Lost Consciousness).

"Who cares when Christ was born anyway?" I imagine announcing once my older sis is alert enough to roll her eyes.

Come April 5th, however, day three of unconsciousness, an additional foreboding symptom kills my hopeful inner clown.

At the Stamford Hospital in Connecticut, a half-hour drive from our childhood home, I find Dad grasping his eldest daughter's hands to stop them from twitching near her chest. Mom flanks Céline's face with her palms to stave off head shaking. Our little brother, Damien, clutches ankles.

Before all that uncontrolled movement, I stand—in hospital sanctioned poofy yellow gown, lunch lady hairnet, and rubber gloves—paralyzed.

Perfectly fucking ironic, right?

***

It seemed like a solid plan to chase exorbitant amounts of money after graduating from Georgetown in 2003. After all, with financial independence come freedoms: to buy the "lust" items you doggy-mark in magazines rather than their affordable, knockoff counterparts; to choose restaurants without skimming menus in advance for a sense of cost; to live without parental assistance in a doorman building with countless amenities you'll never exploit (a billiards room and a sauna you don't have time for! Valet service for the automobile-less! Wheelchair access throughout!), but which comfort regardless.

It was also psychologically fulfilling to be one of few women at an elite investment bank. Differentiated by my lean, 5'10" frame, long, blondish ponytail, and immunity from whatever caused universal crotch itching, I counted myself uniquely well-equipped for the gig. In fact, I thrived in the testosterone-imbued, fratastic atmosphere of the bond trading floor. Some masochistic drive in me that harkens back to my early years as a serious gymnast—before I grew, in height or boobs—was revived whenever my boss called me a "fucking dullard" or told me to "remove head from ass." The derision propelled me to work harder. Taking hits and learning how to toe the thin line between impressing one's superiors with peppery insults and offending them with a tad too much sass was good training, I figured—part of growing the tough outer skin I needed to be successful. For as long as I can remember, I wanted to be successful—in the politically incorrect, monetary way that would elevate me above financial concerns and seemed to involve little downside apart from hard work, which had never scared me.

Wall Street was of course the polar opposite path from the one Céline took. After graduating from Columbia in 1999, Céline moved to Arizona to teach at a prep school outside Phoenix with barely a thought about salary. In a few key ways, my sister and I were very much the same, which isn't all that surprising if you know something about environmental impact. We were raised in the same suburban homes in the same safe towns by the same loving parents committed to our education and wellbeing. But for the most part, our interests diverged, which isn't all that surprising either if you know something about birth order. She picked dandelions on the sidelines at soccer games while I rocketed across the field, a top scorer on every team I joined. She played Mozart on the piano with ease while my hands constantly battled the metronome. She was heavy. I was thin. She sat on the south side of the high school cafeteria, with the smokers, goths, and theater kids. I lunched on the north side, with the jocks. Naturally, if Céline didn't care about making money, I would.

"Stick with me, kid, and I'll have you making a million bucks a year by the time you're 30," promised the head of the Government Bond Desk at the conclusion of my summer internship in 2002. His hand never left the knob of the door he leaned against in one of the glass offices lining the city-block wide trading floor while offering me a fulltime job. Without waiting for me to articulate a reply, he trotted back to his desk—too cocky to consider I might react with anything but genuine gratitude, or too eager to spit out the chewing tobacco threatening to drip down his chin and sully his purple Thomas Pink tie, which was propelled forward by a glutton's gut. Wall Street traders operate with a sense of urgency, roughly 25 percent of which is affected, the rest of which is based upon the fact that absence from one's desk, even for a few seconds, can cost the firm millions of dollars. I wanted to radiate that sense of importance. I also wanted the money that came with it—or informed it.

I was one of about twenty interns recruited from top schools to participate in the firm's Fixed Income Sales & Trading internship program, a comprehensive introduction to the Street that involved mastering the concept of FILO (first in, last out), keeping tack of lunch orders, stepping out of the way when someone slammed a phone down in defeat, and not crying. From this crop of unabashedly competitive, money-hungry young neophytes, I was one of three offered employment beginning immediately after graduation.

By the time I officially began my Wall Street tenure, I was completely dedicated to embracing the ranks of traders. The $7,500 signing bonus and $55,000 starting salary (which would be topped off at the end of year one with a $40,000 cash bonus) helped. In my view, traders were commendably forthright about enjoying the fruits of their labor. The classic trader's pomp was accompanied by a brand of self-awareness I admired. What was so bad about belonging to the golf club of your dreams, owning at least one Range Rover, and dropping "hundies" in tips at your favorite bar? When spoken by a gruff, magnificently unapologetic trader, work hard, play hard enchanted as an aphorism. Got a nobler mantra?

It was not until my third year of staring at bid-offer spreads displayed in tiny neon font on six computer screens for 12-hour stints a day that a sense of depletion crept up on me. Rushing to the bathroom one afternoon, lest I miss the most profitable trade of the day, I caught my reflection in the glass wall of a conference room. It occurred to me how ridiculous I looked comporting myself with the purpose of an E.R. doctor. Back at my desk, I tallied how many dinners I'd missed with friends in the name of being in bed by 9:30pm so I could be on my "A-game" by 6:15am. The stack of financial newsletters to the left of my keyboard suddenly looked about as interesting as a pile of memos on the war in Iraq written by beauty contestants. The pack of gum squished in my pocket mocked me. I used to be a social butterfly, too mindful of resembling a camel to develop a pack-a-day gum-chewing habit, too dutiful or civilized or caring to consider screening calls from friends and family members just because I was tired.

In the face of mounting doubt, however, I remembered that my bank account was nowhere near as depleted as I was. And that was the fucking point.

You want to make shitloads of money, I reminded myself as Bonus Day approached in the spring of 2006. In a series of meetings on this annual day of reckoning, Management would reveal each trader's "number." In general, a person's bonus was expected to represent a staggeringly high percentage of their total compensation (base salaries were relatively low by comparison), but the allotment process was maddeningly subjective. There were no formulas or clear-cut rules surrounding compensation, so no one could know for sure what their number would be, no matter their contribution (perceived or real) to the firm. Hence the incendiary mix of uncertainty, envy, and arrogance that permeated the floor year round, and was most pointed on Bonus Day.

At 23 that year, I exited a much-anticipated powwow with my manager clutching a check for $90,000. But that check for a sum the average middle-aged adult doesn't earn in one year—the rectangular piece of paper that was supposed to reignite my commitment to a profession that afforded me Jimmy Choo heels, a Bottega Veneta handbag, and a sense of self worth—turned on me. Instead of wanting that money and the life it promised, I felt handcuffed by it.

Looking to my left and right on the trading floor, I studied row upon row of wealthy professionals. I examined my colleagues' khaki pants, blue dress shirts, and slicked hairdos, then considered their taste for munchkin eating contests between interns and their thinly veiled disdain for anyone richer than they were. I didn't see anyone whose life I wanted. Instead, I saw the "5 missed calls" alert I'd ignored that morning after dismissing, far too easily, the notion that my sister may have been in trouble when she rang repeatedly between 1am and 3am.

Over the last year or so, Mom had grown concerned about Céline. But Mom was a master of hyperbole—a loud radiator was "as disruptive as a shuttle launch," and if she noticed two people reading the same novel in a day, "an epidemic" was underway—so I could dismiss most of her accounts of Céline's progressively "inexcusable" behavior. I figured Céline had simply shown up a few too many minutes late for a few too many lunch dates, and maybe imbibed a few too many cocktails in Mom's presence. My sister was probably struggling a bit and hitting the bottle to compensate, but I had convinced myself that a little dysfunction fit—somewhere between her penchant for lowbrow magazines and Britney Spears concerts on DVD, which she consumed without regard for the pretensions that governed the rest of her life as a Latin teacher turned NYU PhD Classics student. Céline was an overweight over-achiever hardened by life's tough questions. Ephemerally, I had started to sense her slipping, but I had also told myself that her problems could wait—at least until after Bonus Day.

Next, I saw myself at the family dinner table Thanksgiving past, seated across from my tipsy, brown haired sister, who was in the midst of digressing from the main point of a story. "Headlines only, please" I sighed. She stopped right there, rivaling unwarranted abruptness with instantaneous, irrevocable silence.

That unapologetic self-important swagger I so coveted was within reach, but did success on Wall Street mean sucking at life?

I was relieved that night upon confirming that my sister was safe. She had pocket dialed me, she claimed. Still, Patrick Bateman's murderous streak in American Psycho had swiftly become all too relatable. If I didn't do something differently, I feared Wall Street would make me rich and suck me dry simultaneously.

A few weeks later, I called my sister armed with a confession.

"I have to quit this shit," I said. "And I don't have another plan," I added, meekly, knowing that such a move wasn't made by a practical Georgetown graduate raised by insanely reasonable immigrant parents who valued security above all.

"Who needs the Sensible Path, Stinky?" Céline replied without hesitation, surprising me not with unconditional support, but by referencing, for the first time in years, the nickname she'd coined for me as an eighth grade Latin student keen on declining nouns, including my name: Mélanie, Smelanie, Smels, Smelly, Stinky. (In return I had dubbed her Bird, which didn't make any sense, but didn't have to.)

Crying for the first time in too long without fear of looking like a pussy, I answered: "People who wear pocket squares, I guess."

We laughed.

II

Even after years, I'm embarrassingly unaccustomed to the physical manifestations of cirrhosis: flaps of flesh hanging from atrophied arms, bloated midsection and green skin courtesy of a liver that no longer filters bile. In my older sister, these symptoms are downright terrifying—only marginally less bearable than the clumpiness of her deep chestnut colored mane, washed too infrequently during Intensive Care Unit (ICU) stays, and the puke bucket by her side at all times. Equipment listing her vital statistics offers a sorry distraction from the tubes inserted down her throat—one charged with breathing, the other with sucking blood from her abdomen.

Up until day three of unconsciousness, I could still joke with my sister in spite of such grimness. "You sound remarkably similar to a milkshake being slurped through a straw," I would say, wanting so badly to be the type of person who believed she could hear me. That she lay there unable to speak, let alone laugh, didn't matter because humor had long been our way of connecting. Whatever our differences, we had always shared a specific sense of what constituted funny.

With the arrival of incessant seizing, Day Three robs me of the capacity to laugh. More cruelly, those sporadic, impossible-to-watch-without-weeping convulsions eradicate all hope of a future synchronized chuckle with my sister. There will be no more cackling in matching volume and cadence before trailing off into one confluence of a satisfyingly drawn out sigh, I am forced to realize.

"So we're all in agreement?" The doctor asks, his tone not unfeeling, though nauseatingly measured.

***

Of all the habits I acquired while re-acclimating to the world beyond interest rates and stock prices—sleeping past 5am, visiting museums and art galleries, catching up with friends over impromptu drinks, walking everywhere, slowly, and refusing to wear a bra, to name just a few—midweek matinees with my sister were the most rewarding. It felt wonderfully decadent and liberating to go to the movies when we weren't supposed to, alongside senior citizens and kids playing hooky. Beyond bucking an innocuous norm, I looked forward to laughing with Céline at the same moments during any film, usually while the rest of the audience remained silent.

In the fall of 2007, we exited Lars and the Real Girl, an offbeat romantic comedy starring Ryan Gosling, exchanging appreciation for the best scenes in between rubbing our eyes as they adjusted to daylight following 106 minutes of midday darkness. On autopilot, we headed to our favorite Union Square area café.

As I waited for the barista to prepare our drinks, I peered at my sister, who had wisely reserved the last open table while I placed our order. Céline wore jeans, a pink three-quarter length t-shirt and a matching scarf. She carried a weathered brown leather Coach handbag she'd resurrected from Mom's closet and her nails were painted a bubblegum pink ten shades away from acceptable. In my schoolgirl chic plaid skirt, opaque tights, tall boots and tailored top, I felt obnoxiously well put together. But Céline liked it when her Stinky looked cute, and I liked it when my Bird approved of my outfits.

Presented with two cappuccinos instead of espressos, I smiled and said "thank you" regardless. It took several months, but I had rediscovered the value in overlooking small frustrations—in being kind to distracted cashiers and the pushy boutique salespeople no one wants to talk to, but whose livelihoods depend upon engaging customers. One additional moment of thought was all it took to remember that someone else's lot may or may not—it was impossible to know, of course, but acknowledgement of the spectrum of possibilities was key—suck more than mine did. Context couldn't justify assholery, but it made the world's everyday disappointments a whole lot more palatable. Céline would rather drink espresso than cause a commotion anyway.

Struggling to position our beverages on the impossibly tiny circular tabletop, I posed a seemingly random question: "Is Tipping a city in China, Bird?"

In the feat of facial muscle control I could never master, Céline raised one eyebrow. Then she spotted the tip jar next to the register featuring the tagline I'd cited and laughed, invading the place from nook to cranny with mirthful sound waves. Expecting a retort about cow tipping or dim sum, I was surprised to note Céline's suddenly half-serious expression.

"I have something to tell you," she said. A chest inflating, back straightening breath, then: "I'm pregnant."

Uncertain how to react, I concentrated on contorting my face continuously so as not to reveal too much shock (Céline wasn't dating anyone), disgust (neither of us was prudish, but we only spoke freely about sex as it applied to others and I didn't want to picture my sister getting laid), or angst (how would she pay for an abortion?).

"Who's the sperminator?" I eventually managed.

"He's a high school acquaintance," she said, before adding, "it doesn't matter, because no one is ever going to know about this."

"So I assume you're getting it taken care of," I said, but my sister deserved better than a tired euphemism. "You're having an abortion, right?"

"Indeed I am, Stinky."

"Can I hold your hand while they vacuum your uterus?"

"No. And to clarify, 'no one' doesn't exclude Mom and Dad."

Was I *that* much of a secret keeping risk? Annoyed that she didn't want me there, or embarrassed that she hadn't reacted to my ill-timed attempts at levity, I decided to ask the question I already knew the answer to. It had to be blurted.

"Were you wasted when this happened?"

"Yes," she said, in such a way that I regretted the accusation immediately, even though it had proven valid. Only she possessed this confounding power over me.

I was flush with follow-up questions (how drunk had she been, exactly, on the scale of mildly inebriated to blacked out? Was the guy in question handsome? Was it a one-night stand? Was the sex consensual? How far along was she?), but I refrained from prying. Mostly, I didn't want my older sister to regret confiding in me. So I agreed not to say anything to our parents, then redirected the conversation back to its original course.

"What about cow tipping is supposed to be entertaining?" I asked, hoping the non sequitur would annoy her. It didn't.

As she spoke, I recognized the stench on her breath—one that could be mistaken for Listerine by anyone committed to ignorance.

Along the 20-block walk south to Soho, I pictured my sister stumbling into a quasi-random guy's apartment and tearing her clothes off before inviting him to mount her with a creepy come-hither motion of the finger, one eyebrow elevated an inch above the other. As a self-proclaimed "fag hag," Céline typically patronized gay clubs with her close male friends, so we rarely went out together at night. Was it admirable, the abandon with which she partied her face off? Or was it pathetic? As a functioning PhD student, could she even qualify as self-destructive? *You've made your share of bad, drunken decisions*, I remind myself. And it's not as if an abortion is a bad thing. If Céline didn't want to involve me in the process, I had to respect that. I had plenty of my own shit to figure out anyway.

At home, I grabbed my stash of unpaid bills, which seemed larger by a heavy dose of steroids than when I had last bothered to confront it. I logged onto Chase.com and stared at my dwindling savings account, thinking about how hard it would be to pay the following month's rent. Then I thought about the perils of not having medical insurance. Then, how tedious it must be for prostitutes to pretend they derive pleasure from sucking strangers' dicks.

Making no money had inevitably started to suck. I don't care if you own a yoga mat, blend your own green juices, or have a Master's in Feng Shui. It's frustrating to adjust from making hundreds of thousands of dollars a year to earning zero dollars an hour pursuing sanity and happiness. The shock proved demoralizing, even after reverting to the habits that had gotten me through college, like stealing handfuls of Splenda packets with every coffee purchase and "forgetting" to return borrowed clothing.

I knew I craved something more than selling hundreds of millions of bonds to the Central Bank of China before buying them back slightly cheaper in the open market. But what constituted *more*? Was it ridiculously idealistic to believe one's job shouldn't have to be so much work?

Roughly three desperate thoughts away from setting up a live webcam so I could charge people to watch me masturbate, Billy Ray Cyrus' melodic southern drawl caught my attention. Though I rarely listened to it, I left the TV on for the charade of constant company. "Do what you love, and you'll never work a day in your life," proclaimed Cyrus during the E! True Hollywood

Story about daughter Miley. Though delivered by a One Hit Wonder turned infamous Stage Dad, the message resonated.

Since leaving Wall Street, I had exempted one category from my budgeting initiatives: books. I could barely afford the apartment in which I kept them, but I had collected enough books to make anyone doubt the future of digital publishing. It was as if a certain part of my brain had been neglected while crunching numbers for three straight years. I *needed* to read—classics, contemporary fiction, popular nonfiction, memoirs, even cookbooks. Finally free from school syllabi to select whatever I wanted, bookstores intimidated me with their stacks and stacks of content across categories ripe for consumption. And the more I read, the more I yearned to express myself. The first time I opened a blank Word document with the intention of writing, I felt like a novice Elvis impersonator stepping onto the stage dressed like the King without the right sideburns. But the words came.

I wasn't an English major in college, but my brother, sister and I each developed a solid grasp of grammar from listening to our French immigrant parents speak textbook English. It's ingrained in me to begin restaurant orders with "may I please have" (a phrase that seeks permission) rather than "can I have" (which alludes to ability). And my inner nerd chuckles when people say "I feel badly" since they believe they're being proper while declaring, unknowingly, that their physical sense of touch is impaired. Céline, who embraced languages early on, corrected everyone's grammar at the dinner table. Though I'd sigh whenever she pointed out a split infinitive or a sentence ending in a preposition, I secretly enjoyed knowing these rules, which were violated constantly by so many. There was something empowering about speaking correctly, at least to dorky kids who were taught that education is paramount.

In my case, the downside of being raised in our family was that I've always been hyper aware of my cognitive inadequacies. Céline was The Smart One. I was The Athletic One. Damien was The Compassionate One. As if I didn't already understand this distinction by the fifth grade, my older sister cemented it in my consciousness the day I officially joined Challenge, our school's gifted and talented program. (Trust an intellectual elitist to have ironic timing.)

Standing proudly next to Céline at the bus stop, not even my giant cobalt L.L. Bean backpack could weigh me down. "I'm so excited to be pulled out of class," I told my sister, because exiting the regular classroom to pursue special projects with fellow seedling overachievers was the mark of being a Challenge student. Céline had been participating in the program for years and I wanted her to confirm how cool it was to abandon the masses. With a kick of gravel, Céline replied, "It's great that you got in. Mom had to work really hard for it." All I could say was, "Butthead."

The most devastating part about Céline's comment was that it had to be true. The workbooks and flashcards Mom had "gifted" me with over the summer adopted a putrid new meaning.

When the bus arrived, I took the first available seat next to another kid, but my attempt at defiance begat a second unwelcome realization: Céline was happy to be freed from the pressure to sit with her younger sibling.

Could she have known that her opinion mattered to me above all?

Moments after beginning to indulge Billy Ray Cyrus inspired visions of the writing life, my intellectual self-doubt chip vibrated aggressively. I was never the best writer in my grade, let alone family. Who the fuck was I to just decide to be a writer? I just split an infinitive in my motherfucking (cliché alert!) train of thought! The prospect of trying seemed to promise more embarrassment than fulfillment. So I shoved those obnoxious, unopened bills in the back of my top desk drawer where they could gather dust next to reminders that I was due for a dental cleaning. Then I changed the channel.

***

When Mom called a few weeks later, I figured she wanted to check, for the bazillionth time, whether I'd purchased a Catastrophic Health Insurance Plan, which, at the cost of a few hundred bucks a year, covers policyholders in the event of an unprecedented health crisis. Maternal persistence made me feel snuggly and exasperated at the same time, an emotional coupling I wasn't usually eager to field. But a glance at the clock confirmed that Mom and Céline should have been on a flight to Colorado, where they planned to visit the Grand Canyon, so I answered.

News of this trip, which Mom intended as a proactive, one-on-one intervention of sorts, had come as a massive relief. I doubted it would be hard for Céline to curb her drinking once confronted by our mother, who was notoriously as straightforward and strict as she was loving. When they returned, Céline and I could exchange jokes about Mom's decision to confront a gaping wide abyss of a problem before Nature's most awe-inspiring geological cavity. *Life is a rocky ravine: One too many missteps and you'll tumble, headfirst, all the way down!* Céline would come up with something cleverer.

"What's up?" I said, "Flight delayed?"

Mom's eerie response: "Security stopped us, Mélanie."

One thousand percent certain I didn't want to know more, I asked what happened.

"Your sister was too bombed to board the plane. We have to wait for the next flight out. This is bad, Mélanie."

"Maybe she's looped from a Xanax," I suggested.

Part of me was annoyed at Mom for sounding somewhat humiliated instead of purely concerned. Another part of me automatically jumped to my sister's defense because I owed her for the time she unknowingly took the fall for me back in the third grade. Doesn't a lifelong tally of Karmic debits and credits govern all sibling relationships?

***

"Mélanie! Céline! Downstairs now," Mom commanded.

I was normally Mél or Mél-Mél, so my full name spelled trouble. With each step toward the entryway, I mulled over the recent behavioral blunders for which I might be getting punished. Céline's frantic expression told me she was doing the same.

In ankle length skirt, blouse, and flats, Mom paused, refusing to reveal the source of her anger—perhaps hoping for a confession, perhaps torturing us on purpose.

"Follow me," she eventually ordered.

Terrified, we marched into the candelabra- and antique- spotted living room area reserved for cocktail and coffee hours. Mom stopped before her walnut secretary, hands on hips forming triangles at her sides, like a peacock in heat, though her expanded frame signified rage. On top of the desk sat an old-timey inkwell punctured by a pheasant feather I often imagined in the hand of a monk wearing a cloak like one I had seen in Robin Hood.

"Who did this?" She asked, pointing to the forest green leather covering the desktop.

Not until I saw the block letters etched there reading "Old King Cole" did I remember inscribing them with my fingernail a week earlier, mid-daydream. I had seen a movie by that title in school featuring an era past, so it fit that I'd recollect it while leaning against Mom's secretary alongside my imaginary monk friend. Unfortunately, the parchment with burnt edges on which I'd envisioned scribbling a secret message was in fact green leather. I never intended to ruin Mom's fancy furniture, but I couldn't bear the thought of disappointing her by fessing up, so I shook my head.

"Not me either," Céline said.

"Someone had to have done this. Someone destroyed my secretary. And someone will be punished," said Mom, French accent thickened by fury.

Neither of us spoke as Mom's eye slits darted from one suspect child to the other.

"You're grounded, Céline. For two weeks," she declared.

"But I didn't do anything!" Céline protested.

"Go upstairs. Both of you."

Céline was likely blamed because this was more her kind of mess than mine. Maybe to compensate for being less bright, I was the kid with the museum neat room who volunteered to help set the table and rake the front lawn. Céline, on the other hand, had less regard for order. Piles of clothing accumulated in corners of her bedroom, she left wrappers everywhere, and she had a knack for breaking things when emptying the dishwasher.

I didn't feel good about allowing my sister to take the fall, but to say that I felt overly remorseful would be a stretch since I never admitted fault. My guilt over the whole thing only flared up when I possessed some amount of power to protect my sister from Mom's anger.

***

"Her pores are oozing booze, Mélanie. I can smell it."

Sibling loyalty was no match for Mom's olfactory prowess. This time, she'd pinpointed the right culprit. Or had she? Was alcohol to blame, or Céline?

Up until this point, the changes in Céline had been relatively contained—sufficient to warrant a sit-down with Mom disguised as a vacation, but probably imperceptible to those who didn't know her well. My sister's most notable offenses to date had involved showing up late to family gatherings, or showing up suspiciously blitzed. There was also the time she bailed on Maid of Honor duty the day of a friend's wedding, but that move was so bizarre that it struck others as a normal misfortune. She must have been seriously ill, they figured. She wasn't. Beyond that, the surest sign of trouble was her acute phobia of the future. Whenever I asked my sister what her plans were—that general question that rolls off the tongue during so many conversations—she would look at me as if I'd asked her to decapitate a baby seal. The very idea of the future—near or far—visibly pained her. I always changed the subject, because it seemed cruel not to. I could also relate. Is there a way to differentiate growing pains from the clinically depressive sort? Overall, I had come to view Céline as a person who drank way too much, but who managed to function—to take classes, ace exams, and spit wit like always.

Getting too drunk to board a plane with Mom midday warranted a new level of concern. For the first time, someone outside our family unit had recognized Céline's out-of-control behavior—and acted on it. An airline ticket collector actualized my sister's issues. Still, I was unprepared to accept this undeniable evidence that my sister was anything but mostly okay. As different as we were, I considered her a role model, still worthy of emulation. What the fuck was I supposed to do about it all? I wasn't an authority on addiction. That word—addict—seemed too serious a label to slap on my sister just yet anyway. Or was it?

"I'll speak to Céline when you guys get back," I said. "She needs to go to rehab."

Still pacing after our call, I thought about my sister. She excelled at every academic subject without trying hard because she was so fucking smart. It aggravated me that she was wasting her brain. It was offensive, almost, because she was exponentially more capable than I was. Or was she? What the fuck is talent worth if untapped? For reasons beyond my control—a series of genetic and environmental accidents separate from those that governed my sister's existence—I was programmed with self-control, ambition, and the will to take risks.

Suddenly, the only thing more ridiculous than trying to be a writer was *not* trying. Maybe I wasn't supposed to be a writer, but I wanted to be one. Wasn't that enough?

Propelled by ire, injustice, and determination to distract myself, I headed to McNally Jackson, an independent bookstore with an adjacent café where Céline and I often met, to make my first look-the-writerly-part purchase: a Moleskin notepad. Inside, I inscribed my first goal: to be published by the humor website McSweeney's Internet Tendency because 1.) The founder, David Eggers, wrote A Heartbreaking Work of Staggering Genius, the first novel I read out of Wall Street and 2.) They accepted random submissions. Through reading online forums about the industry, I knew I needed credits to my name to get published. The only way to resolve this chicken-or-egg type conundrum was to write for a site like McSweeney's for free, which sounded completely absurd to my inner Wall Streeter. Then again, guaranteed misery in perpetuity had to be more absurd than a chance, however miniscule, at eventual career contentment.

Later, while applying for several credit cards at zero percent interest, I realized how good it felt to have a plan. On the last page of my Moleskin, I even scribbled a Motherfucking Backup Plan: If writing doesn't work out, there's still time to Trophy Wife your way to stability (at the cost of 75 to 90 percent of your dignity).

***

After being stood up several weeks in a row, the sight of my sister waiting outside Café Gitane, our favorite French Moroccan restaurant in downtown Manhattan, startled. She was as much a contradiction as the Menthol cigarette—at once minty fresh and destructive—she flicked to the gutter before bear-hugging me.

"You look healthy and happy! In case I haven't said it enough: It's really great to have you back, Stinky."

Increasingly frustrated by my financial situation, I welcomed this reminder as to why I'd left Wall Street. It changed me for the worse, and Céline probably intuited that long before I did. Growing up, I began every school year with a teacher who had already instructed my sister. Adults and peers revered her for her sharp wit, indiscriminate compassion, and insightfulness. She paved the way for me. She never had quite the right haircut or outfit, but Céline could belt out Cat Stevens at exactly the right moment to make a girl who cared too much about the right outfit smile. She knew me. Why couldn't I leave the serious talk up to Mom and Dad? It was their responsibility, wasn't it? I was the little sister. Céline had promised Mom that she would change while they were in Colorado. Did she really need me to suggest rehab?

By the time our appetizers arrived, any resentment I felt toward Céline had evaporated.

The Law of Siblings dictated that our relationship was never more than a few milliseconds of warmth beyond repair, even under the worst circumstances.

"Any special guys in your life?" Céline asked.

"Guys require energy I'm not ready to expend."

Céline nodded. "Probably best to find Mélanie before searching for Mister Right."

She had a way of articulating things about me I hadn't even pinpointed quite yet. Tempted as I was in that moment to inquire about her own man plan—to assess where we were on the Richter scale by introducing that explosive, forward-looking word—I held back. Perhaps sensing my internal debate, Céline stood to go to the bathroom before it was too late. The clanking of keys against glass bottle from within her purse sounded then like the fire alarm for a mandatory drill we both longed to ignore.

Immediately, I regretted sparing her *plan's* volcanic potential. I considered how to address that pesky noise—to clarify that she wasn't fooling me. For instance, I might ask whether there was an Oompa Loompa clamoring for help in there. That was the kind of nonsensical reference to our youth that would typically makes us both laugh, so its potential for impact was great. But this wasn't a joke. My admirable sister was retreating to the restroom in the middle of dinner for an extra swig of vodka, or three. I was supposed to do something. But what? Humiliate her? Reprimand her? Play the bigger sister?

Our eyes, behind which rested boundless reservoirs of memories—good and bad, beautiful and ugly, exaggerated and understated—challenged each other. My lips didn't move. Hers did.

"Why do you always assume the worst in me?" she asked.

The last time Céline made me feel this powerless, she was 14, and she had lice.

***

From Céline's bedroom doorway, in white ruffled pajamas dotted with pink hearts, I watched my sister scratch her head feverishly while finishing homework—the easy kind, I knew, since The Bangles blasted in the background. At 11 I had homework too, but no matter how old I got, my life was perpetually less interesting than hers. She wore a nightgown and our grandfather's brown striped robe, which he'd given to her as soon as she'd noted that it "looked properly loved and lived in." It was a dreadful piece of clothing and I didn't envy it, but I did envy my sister's ability to be fond of such a decrepit thing. I was also jealous of the summers Céline spent in France visiting our relatives, mastering the Berliet's native tongue. The one time I accompanied her for three weeks out of eight, I became unbearably homesick and spent hours crying in various bathrooms, terrified that I couldn't call to mind every contour of Mom's face, as if my inability to do so meant that she might spontaneously vaporize. Céline thrived during her solo visits to Europe, reveling in the change in scenery, the Nutella toasts dunked into chocolat chaud, and the attention of cousins, aunts, uncles, and grandparents. I was a baby when it came to adapting to new circumstances, maybe because I was so damn at peace in my existing situation. Reinvention isn't something the satisfied seek, is it?

"Come here," Céline said when she noticed me hovering. "I'll check your head."

Such bedroom hospitality was rare, so I usually welcomed it. But this time I didn't budge, grossed out by the idea of tiny insects feeding off my scalp, certain that nearing my sister would guarantee the infestation of my lovely, bug free locks. Whether more disgusted or scared, I was unprepared for what came next.

In response to my hesitation, Céline screamed, "I'm not a monster!" Then she flung her chewed up black Bic pen at my face.

Though I ducked in time to avoid the plastic missile, I couldn't back away from the torment I had caused. Confused and horrified by my sister's reaction, I acquiesced to inspection.

Two days later, the school nurse sent me home with lice.

***

Non-confrontational by nature, I've always avoided conflict, even by admitting fault to end a fight when I believe I'm right. Céline knew this. Was she manipulating me into submission? How was it possible to be controlled by someone so obviously out of control?

Subconsciously or not, as soon as she returned from the ladies' room, I diverted the conversation. "I want to be a writer," I blurted. "But I've already been rejected by McSweeney's *ten* times. It's pathetic. I'm the Steve Baldwin of the writing world—doomed to embarrass myself trying to make it at something my sibling's naturally better at. I should probably give up and become a Jesus Freak already."

As Céline reached for a roll, I realized how validated I felt simply because she wasn't mocking me. I knew to let her think undisturbed. Did I know my sister as well as she knew me? While Céline buttered and pondered, I considered the glaze coating her eyes. It was transparent, but impossible to see through.

Finally, "McSweeney's is a humor website, right?"

"Yup."

"Why the fixation with publishing humor, and with McSweeney's in particular?"

I hadn't expected Céline to shower me with accolades about my innate talent, but I hadn't expected such drunken insight, either. Her point was basic, but perceptive. I had limited myself through preoccupation with an arbitrary goal. Humor writing was a specialization, so I should start simpler. And I could pitch anyone. I didn't have to start with such a prestigious outlet.

A few bites into her Shepherd's Pie, perhaps clutching the coattails of the newfound resolve she'd instilled in me, Céline revealed her own news: "I've decided a PhD is superfluous, Stinky."

"You mean you quit school?!"

"I'm going to be a nanny for a family with two delightful toddlers. They live uptown."

I knew Céline had grown frustrated by academia, but I never guessed she would abandon her doctorate. What about those beloved classmates and professors? The scholarly esteem? The stipend? Mom and Dad would be aghast. But how could I not support my sister as she'd supported me when I left Wall Street?

"I guess a toast is in order," I said, handicapped by past benevolence. Then I ordered the round of drinks I'd cornered myself into. What else was there to do?

After paying the bill and handing my sister the $40 she needed to buy a birthday cake for a friend,

I walked across town and sat on a bench overlooking the Hudson River. It was cold out, but I envisioned Céline, myself, and Céline's old friend Kelly in the backyard of our childhood home.

***

On the first summer day of 1989 hot enough to warrant backyard sprinkler action the three of us stood, eagerly waiting for Mom to set up our makeshift water park. I wore a hand-me-down one-piece bathing suit with purple zigzags and ties at the sides. Céline wore a similarly conservative black number that would one day be mine. Kelly, at 11 a year older than Céline and four years my senior, strutted around in a two-piece. When Mom finally twisted the knob connected to the garden hose, dotted lines of water spurted higher and higher. We cheered.

"Remember, no one re-enters the house without a towel," Mom warned before ditching her gloves to head indoors. "I'm making croque monsieur for lunch."

Céline, Kelly and I took turns dashing through the cool curtain of moisture, enjoying our simple fun. As I embarked on my tenth or so run, however, Kelly took it upon herself to spice things up. Fake microphone to mouth, voice an octave lower than usual, she announced: "Here comes

Mélanie Berliet. Today she wears a lilac suit. At about four feet tall, she's supermodel skinny. Watch those chicken legs as she goes. But don't get any ideas, boys! Word has it, she'll break your heart." In that moment, I felt truly special—the center of a cool kid's cool game. I watched Céline take off toward the sprinkler, smiling in anticipation of the next round of commentary. "And here comes Céline, the first born Berliet," Kelly began. With a vampish flip of her hair, "At four feet, eight inches, Céline weighs about…a ton and a half! She's the Miss Piglet of her family and the entire fifth grade!"

Céline's trot became a walk as my heart caved in. Never had I known the bitterness of excitement soured so quickly. Once, Mom let me try a handful of promotional popcorn at the grocery store and I was horrified to discover the pungency of mustard in place of buttery goodness. Angry at that popcorn for ambushing my taste buds, I swore the snack off for months. The feeling overwhelming me in the yard was far more nauseating, though. In staccato, a series of grating realizations: people viewed Céline as fat; even "friends" made fun of her; and I was a pawn in Kelly's wicked game. Yes, Céline was chubby. Yes, I was guilty of teasing her too. But Kelly existed outside the cocoon of sisterhood.

"Shut up, Kelly," Céline shouted, then curled her short brown hair behind both ears and wrapped herself in one of the towels laid out on the deck. "Lunch is probably ready," she said on her way in, feet speckled with segments of freshly mown grass.

I followed. The vicarious hurt overwhelming me was love, I knew.

***

Without question, I loved my sister. But things were so much more complicated than when I could trail her inside to demonstrate support. It hit me how easily I'd been duped into handing my sister cash to buy "a cake" after dinner. Was she kicked out of the PhD program because she could no longer hack it? Was she ever pregnant?

In my sister's presence, I was so fucking malleable. A coward. Play-Doh. One sincere look from her and I transformed into a child unwilling to risk upsetting my older sister to address the issue at hand.

As if things weren't fucked up enough, while I failed to assist my sister she had managed to motivate me. I was ready to double my efforts and to broaden my approach towards writing. From my phone, I reread one of the many canned rejection emails I'd received from the Editor in Chief of McSweeney's: "This one's not a good fit for us. Thank you for submitting." I had worked hard to generate those terse sentences, but the only thing to do was to try again, and to try elsewhere. I needed to spend yet less money and to network more vigilantly. While my sister squandered her gifts, I would capitalize on my inferior ones. If the world favored me, it did so unjustly. Whatever the case, my sister's reluctance or inability to figure her shit out somehow mandated that I did.

Pajama clad, I resurrected my stash of unpaid bills and recorded amounts due in a spreadsheet. I surfed Craiglist for part-time work. Then I did something I'd thought about but chickened out of repeatedly. I emailed Mike Sacks, an author and Vanity Fair staffer: "Thank you for being awesome. I love your work." An honest, un-intrusive message.

Sacks responded within minutes, which told me that the Universe wanted him to be my Miyagi. I considered texting my sister as much but decided against it.

III

The crevices between Céline's straight white teeth, the sole physical trait about which she boasted regularly, are blood stained. Is it best she'll never know this?

Doc continues, "The way we'll go about this—the way that should be the least painful for Céline—is to stop administering her blood pressure medicine. Without it, her blood won't flow."

I hate the doctor for addressing my sister by name—for trying to sound personal or make us feel comfortable. I don't need a medical professional to soften the truth at hand: alcoholic-turned-vegetable on life support, prognosis bad.

Céline doesn't need that bullshit, either. Too modest to think her life grand, my sister never feared death. She feared dying. Of physical pain, she was always afraid. Of bees. Of dogs. Of needles. The latter dread we actually shared. "At least we'll never be heroin junkies!" we used to exclaim.

How the fuck did we go from joking about addiction to dying from it?

***

By the time things were going well in the summer of 2008, "going well" meant that Céline hadn't been hospitalized for an alcohol related incident in weeks. Funny how expectations change. Bringing home an A-minus used to be the only way she disappointed. Now, a 30-day period free from collapsing in public was an accomplishment. Much to the dismay of my parents, who had invested large sums in Céline's Ivy League education, their eldest genuinely enjoyed nannying. Should I have been grateful to my sister for lowering the bar she once held so high? Even if I never made it as a writer, I wouldn't be a drunken fuck-up.

To avoid pauperdom, I took a part-time position as an administrator at a company that organized conferences. I was also reviewing shops, bars and restaurants for a few blogs as often as possible, earning a fee comparable to what Mom and Dad once paid me hourly to rake leaves. On the upside of exhausting synonyms for "delicious" and "chic," I was racking up bylines. Though thousands of dollars in debt, I managed to stay up to date on minimum monthly payments.

My credit was probably still good enough to purchase a four-bedroom home somewhere in the heartland, thereby providing some trader yet another mortgage to slap into the tranche of a complex securitized product to be bought and sold, and bought and sold, and bought and sold. It sucked to conform to an office dress code again for half the week, but wearing sensible blouses probably beat touching myself in front of a live web cam for money, and it definitely beat going back to Wall Street. Luckily, I had mastered the alt-tab keyboard trick so I could write most of the day and switch screens without moving hand to mouse whenever my superiors passed by. To have no superiors—that was the dream.

While dressing one morning, it hit me that I no longer needed half the clothes hanging in my closet, most of which I'd amassed during my trading years. The pricey duds were a badge of sorts, but one I no longer needed. I stuffed them into a giant shopping bag and headed straight to a thrift store.

As a staffer evaluated a $450 Elie Tahari dress I once considered corporate cool, an old Wall Street colleague, Buck, rang out of the blue.

"Dinner. Tonight. Me and the guys. Cipriani," he said. "Downtown."

The abruptness of Buck's delivery was familiar in spite of distance, and not entirely unwelcome. Was I nostalgic, or just hungry? I wanted no part in reprising my role as Token Female, or witnessing a group of adult men chart the relative firmness of waitresses' asses. But I was in no position to turn down a free meal, so I accepted, laughing off the irony of Buck's timing in conjunction with my grand farewell to cashmere sweater sets.

**

Cipriani's Downtown is a restaurant that's lit so diners can see and be seen. Determined to enjoy the costly fare, I managed to smile as the guys questioned me. "So what's life as a poor person like?"

"How long before you grow out of this boho thing and beg to blow one of us to get your job back?"

"Who'd you wanna bang most back in the day, anyway?" someone asked after "whiskey numero tres."

I was too distracted to answer, though, entranced by a tall guy who had swaggered into the restaurant one slow motion moment before, in a white blazer and dark jeans. He was strikingly handsome, though unconventionally so, and his arrogance, while palpable from a distance, was somehow not off-putting. In his case, the line between cocky and self-assured seemed properly blurry. With a nod and a wink, he passed the hostess without checking in. Marching onward, he dodged bus boys and waitresses with precision, stopping once in a while to put hand to chest and bow ten degrees in apology for grazing a table. He was so poised, I wondered if the table grazing was on purpose. When he took the empty seat next to mine, I was stupefied. My mystery man didn't fit in with the slick haired penguins badgering me with uncouth questions.

Hand outstretched, the enigma spoke: "Sasha. Short for Alexandre," he said.

"Really?"

"That's how the Russian's abbreviate," he shrugged. "Alexandre is actually my middle name. First name's Serguei, but I ditched that when the kids started calling me 'Sir Gay' back in elementary school."

I reckoned Sasha was in the habit of dousing things as ordinary as introductions with a hint of special.

"I'm—"

"Mélanie." In response to my obvious confusion, "I always ask Buck who he's inviting to dinner when I get him a reservation." Leaning in closer than etiquette permits a typical stranger, "Said he'd *locked down* a girl called Mélanie."

I appreciated Sasha's gentle mocking of Wall Street lingo. "I take it you're the owner of this intimate joint?"

"I own another spot in town. To be clear, that was a compliment, Mélanie."

Brazen, but perceptive. Sasha's devilish charm impressed me too much to be irksome. I could have sworn there was a wishing star in each of his twinkling gray-blue eyes. Staring into them, I blushed.

At age six, after watching the summer Olympics, I told Mom I wanted to quit ballet so I could start gymnastics, a sport at which I excelled for years. On my 20th birthday, I tasted my first strawberry after stubbornly dismissing all fruits and vegetables for two decades simply because they didn't look appetizing. To this day, I've spurned threats from dentists and refused to stop sucking my thumb. Whichever unequivocal sense of knowing guided me in these respects resounded within minutes of meeting Sasha. I *knew* I wanted the man.

The rest of the table didn't exist as Sasha and I launched into an accelerated get to-know-you session through which we learned that we were both first generation Americans, and that we shared an over-appreciation for Scrabble, the Discovery Channel and Smores. Sasha proved interested in my writerly ambitions, making me promise to email him samples of my work. By the end of dinner, I treasured his quirks: the stroking of buzzed head when pensive, the request for a lowball "peasant glass" from which to drink his wine, and the pursing of lips when most would furrow their brow.

Hours later, while setting up the board for a game of strip Scrabble at Sasha's office, which was abandoned for the weekend and resembled an apartment more than a workplace, I noticed the wedding band. Fuck, I thought. Not one to fantasize about bridal gowns, a dance with Dad, or tables peppered with just the right assortment of votives, ring-finger focus wasn't one of my automatic settings. In the last couple years especially, I'd grown less and less certain that a traditional family unit would suit me. I used to long for motherhood, but now I felt troubled by the idea that a person had no say in their own creation. I often found myself wondering whether it was okay to invite life on another human. Still, I wasn't quite hardened enough to disregard the implications of involvement with a married man. Or was I? Boyfriending Sasha immediately and cohabiting after a three-month whirlwind love fest wasn't feasible. Neither was not sleeping with him.

In Sasha's company, I felt whole from minute one—emotionally, intellectually and sexually. Normally it takes time to learn a lover's body, but Sasha and I needed no help locating each other's pleasure buttons. Being with him felt natural, necessary, normal. Like two halves of a pretzel with Transformer properties, our bodies moved from one interlocked position into the next. He was equally tender and vigorous. When I mounted him backwards to assume the "reverse cowgirl" position on a whim, he said I'd read his mind. "Spank me!" I screamed. Was Sasha's confidence contagious? Like my sister's fuck-it way of life? Was everything contagious, or was I just that impressionable?

As Sasha and I chatted in post coital bliss—about everything from Banksy's graffiti to the increasingly popular trend of naked body sushi modeling—I determined to ignore the pesky ring once and for all. There was life in our passion and relinquishing that seemed wrong. I didn't need a typical romance. I needed him.

"I'd write about that whole sushi weirdness," I said, "but the story's been covered to death already."

"No one's written it from the model's perspective," Sasha countered.

"Are you suggesting I let strangers eat sushi rolls off my naked body?" I asked, reaching to pluck a tiny gray hair from the scant patch of dark brown fur blanketing his chest.

"Ay!" he said, instead of "ow," like any good European would. "Exactly. That's a story!"

To combat the all too predictable emptiness that set in after bidding Sasha farewell, I did what any self-respecting gal in my position would do: I Googled his wife. Within seconds, dozens of party pictures populated my computer screen. She was beautiful, but most importantly, she looked strikingly similar to me. It might make sense for Sasha to have a type—tall, thin blondes with pointed noses and small faces—but the resemblance unsettled nonetheless. The only logical thing to do was scrutinize her for flaws. So I clicked from image to image, checking out her legs, which looked thicker than mine in several frames, and then her boobs, which seemed smaller than mine. It was obvious she had a wardrobe full of expensive clothing, which annoyed me, but her style in combination with a few key wrinkles told me that she was five to ten years older. I deconstructed the innocent woman until I was left feeling appropriately terrible for attacking someone I didn't know with a superficial sword. Is there anything less attractive?

I knew nothing about Sasha's wife, and I knew nothing about their marriage. All I could do was make semi-educated guesses based upon Sasha's vague account. But I knew deep down that you can't trust the words of a guy who wants to get in your pants. I wanted to believe that Sasha's marriage was troubled, but people often cheat for no reason other than to fulfill a fleeting sexual desire. Maybe Sasha and his wife had wardrobes lined with coordinated clothing and referred to each other by some adorable term of endearment that made sense only to them, like "butch." Maybe it was irrational and reckless to let myself fall for a married man, even if I knew I could—already did, maybe—love him.

In a frenzy, I closed every window picturing Sasha's wife. Uncertain what to do with myself, I called Céline to review the sushi concept. Even if I never saw Sasha again, I had gained a memory and a potentially great idea.

Straight to voicemail. My sister never turned her phone off, but it had died on the occasions she was hospitalized for severe drunkenness.

On autopilot, detached from a world in which the gratification of knowing Sasha and the challenge of becoming a writer existed, I rang my parents. Céline had been admitted to St. Vincent's in the middle of the night, they confirmed. A stranger had discovered her passed out on the subway platform. Extensive bruising indicated a mugging. Her blood-alcohol level indicated obliteration.

I threw on a pair of yoga pants and a t-shirt, but as I turned the front doorknob, something from within petitioned me to sit back down at my desk. Compared to the ER scene ahead, the idea of playing human serving platter barely seemed like a test. In a flurry of what-the-fuck conviction, I drafted a pitch to my new Vanity Fair friend, Mike Sacks, with the subject "Confessions of a Naked Body Sushi Model." It didn't matter what anyone might think. We're all equally insignificant in the grander scheme. Why not decide for myself what was acceptable, and what wasn't? Why ask why when the better question was clearly why not?

**

At Saint Vincent's, I waved to the receptionist in the lobby. I hated that I could locate the ICU ward without asking for directions; hated the stench of sickness layered with sterilizing chemicals; hated the nervous, inexperienced visitors crowding my elevator; hated the doctors with their scrubs and their Hippocratic oath, which prevented them from speaking to me about my sister's condition just because she'd ordered them not to; hated myself for hating it all.

It's easy to pile hate upon hate—until you find your sister sitting on a makeshift toilet in her assigned room, saggy breasts peeking through haphazardly tied gown. How many wore that cheap medical frock before her? How many times had that cotton endured the spin cycle and an industrial iron?

Céline said nothing, allowing me to stand back and look away as she finished her business and climbed back onto her bed. How long would it take her to fall asleep on such stiff sheets? The whites of her eyes were grass stained and the mound of her bloated stomach contrasted rail thin arms. She looked like an injured pigeon abandoned by its flock, with nothing to do but limp from crack to crack on the sidewalk. Does anyone ever bother to rescue a street bird?

"Hey, Stinky," Céline said, barely audible. The sadness seeping through each strained syllable made mulch out of whatever plan I'd conjured during the taxi ride over.

"Hey," I said, because that's what the moment called for.

Then I took my perch on the windowsill and waited for my sister to find something watchable on television. As she clicked, I recalled the first time she seemed fragile to me.

***

Céline, Damien, Dad and I sat in the front pew of St. Aloysius for Sunday mass. (Our Atheist mother never joined us at church, but she supported her children's exposure to religion so we could make informed decisions about whether or not to worship in adulthood.) As the priest concluded his homily and signaled the band, Dad opened his hymnal. Normally, Céline and I would exchange glances to poke fun at our tone-deaf father's off-key warbling. But when I looked at Céline, wearing classic navy blue slacks instead of the jeans on most teens, I saw that she was shaking while staring straight ahead, fixated on something I couldn't detect.

I tugged the sleeve of Dad's blazer. Before he could scold me for disturbing his rhythm, he noticed Céline's odd behavior.

"Are you okay, sweetheart?" he asked.

But Céline wouldn't, or couldn't, answer. She fainted.

Mass was halted. Concerned, well-dressed ladies rushed toward us. An ambulance came.

Weren't Céline and I devouring smoked turkey sandwiches on neighboring stools a few hours earlier? What could have provoked her meltdown? The melee was truly dumbfounding.

Later, it was determined that Céline had suffered a panic attack. While my sister rested on the family room couch, I gazed at her from the adjacent chair, annoyed by what I considered an unnecessary detour to Crazy Town. As a preadolescent, I associated pain with circumstance—the stuff that comprised the plots of late night TV movies I wasn't supposed to stay up to watch. Widowers deserved to feel sad. So did the homeless, the handicapped and the orphaned. My sister and I led a cushy suburban existence. What could possibly be so bad?

Without any effort to mask exasperation, I asked "What exactly are you so anxious about?"

But Céline couldn't, or wouldn't, answer. In response to my cruelty, she wept.

I sat back, unwilling to apologize—also, unwilling to leave her side.

***

In my sister's presence, I could sense the darkness lying beneath her infectious, jocular exterior. I knew the grim stuff she was compelled to drown existed, and whatever darkness she harbored didn't scare me. But the prospect of upsetting my older sister did. I didn't want to pose a question that would make her shut down, or demand that I leave. I didn't want to compromise our effortless, irreplaceable sisterlyness. If the alternative to enabling was alienating, was there a right choice?

Instead of diving into a waterfall muddied with condescending questions, at the commercial break I told my sister about the sushi concept.

"I feel like sushi," Céline whimpered.

"For dinner?"

"No," she said. "I feel like a fish out of water...here."

"Everyone feels that way at the hospit—"

"No. Here...on Earth."

During middle school, Céline would venture off on absurdly long walks with only a Walkman for company. This frustrated me because walking fast in silence sounded totally un-fun. I also wanted her around—and for her to want to be around. "I need to think," she'd retort whenever I begged her to stay. "About what?" I would plead. And the answer was always the same: "The meaning of life." Céline was constantly contemplating and I was constantly trying to distract her—because that's what bratty little sisters do, and because I felt, on some level, that it was my duty to.

"Then fuck the surf! Let's go out for some turf this week. My treat."

A near imperceptible hint of a laugh. Mission accomplished.

In the midst of bonding, it felt natural—necessary, even—to admit everything about my tryst with Sasha.

"He makes you happy," Céline diagnosed. "That's important."

Nothing more.

As always, I walked the 12 or so blocks from St. Vincent's to my Soho studio in silence, without checking my phone, as if paying respects to some higher power I didn't believe in. Only after eating lunch in quiet, I let myself check my email.

A message from an unfamiliar sender, Michael Hogan, had arrived in response to a familiar subject line. Hogan noted that his colleague, Mike Sacks, had forwarded him my sushi pitch and offered me $500 for 1,000 words. Finally, a well-paid assignment for a well-respected publication!

I rang Céline, who had her own announcement: "I'm checking into rehab as soon as I'm healthy enough to be released," she said. She explained that her latest drinking binge occurred after she was fired from her nannying gig. The kids had grown frightened of her increasingly green skin.

"So a couple of toddlers accomplished what no one else could?" I said.

"Indeed they did, Stinky."

"I love you, Bird."

IV

"How long will it take?" Mom asks, voice muffled.

"It's impossible to predict. We'll administer extra Ativan and wait," says the doctor.

"Her organs. Can we donate any?" I stammer, surprising myself with such a silly question. Céline was medicated for years, so none of her organs could be viable. *Like a fish out of water,* I hear her whisper. She had felt ill-equipped. Misplaced.

"Unfortunately none are salvageable," Lab Coat confirms.

"Not even her heart? Or her eyes?" I persist.

A week earlier, I noticed a poster on a Metro-North subway car picturing Vanessa Williams and her brother, both proponents of eye donation since their father had benefited from it. Am I supposed to campaign against alcoholism now? Make myself feel better about Céline's booze-addled existence by nurturing some heartfelt affection for others who suffer from what's killing her? Help them? *What a tedious thought,* I hear my sister say.

"She's been given too much medication. I'm sorry," says Doc.

On cue, a nurse in pinkish scrubs enters. Her name, Marina, is scribbled on the white board at the foot of Céline's bed. Whenever I ran out of jokes during hospital visits, I would doodle on those things. I'd write C-É-L-I-N-E along the left edge and come up with a word beginning with each letter to create an amusing (to us, at least) first grade level poem. For example:

Cause
Eternal
Life
Is
Nonsense,
Enstein

"You're the Yeats of acrostic poetry," Céline once said. I took a strange amount of pride in that.

***

On the eve of my sushi article's publication, Sasha knocked on my door bearing a basket of cheeses and a bottle of champagne, baguette tucked beneath arm.

Upon seeing him, I smiled wide, then wrapped my arms around his neck and kissed him in a prolonged, daytime soap way, purposefully provoking him to shove me aside.

"Where's your beret?" I joked.

"Attendez une minute, s'il vous plait," he said, and went straight to work

As I watched him set up an indoor picnic, deliberately placing each item on my forest green rug, I had to marvel at the fact that I'd met someone as anal as I was.

Around Sasha, I felt like the highest pixelated version of my true self. I never thought about what to say or how to act. There were no hints of phoniness on either side. When we were together, no matter where we were or what we were doing, I knew for certain that I was spending my time in the most rewarding way possible. It didn't matter if I had to upset my routine or patronize a restaurant I wasn't crazy about. When Sasha was part of the equation, I easily abandoned my own wants. Is that what they mean by love with abandon? Merely by being present, Sasha stripped me of concerns and injected me with hope that life could be truly awesome.

What was I supposed to do? Shelve my unshakable need for him in the name of an official piece of paper representing an archaic institution? Wait around for the other piece of paper legalizing his split from his wife? Life seemed way too fucking short. If you have a chance at happiness, aren't you supposed to take it?

I chose to believe that Sasha had married too young, and that he and his wife weren't right for each other. Even if they were right for each other at one point, it seemed they no longer were. The sheer volume of party pictures featuring Sasha's wife (would I ever learn to restrain my Google flexer?) supported the notion that their interests had diverged long ago. She frequented early evening cocktail parties swarming with socialites, in part because her position as a Public Relations executive demanded it, but I surmised that she enjoyed the scene. Meanwhile, Sasha preferred the camaraderie of staffers at his restaurant and group dinners with friends. Or me. Even if Sasha and his wife were still right for each other in some ways, they couldn't possibly be *as* right for each other as we were. This thought process was insufficient, unfair, and illogical, but I didn't care. I didn't need concrete justification, or to believe that what I was doing was "right." I needed to believe in something, and I believed in us.

Sasha and I sipped bubbly and fed each other pieces of cheese encased in truffle honey dipped bread. What would have felt excessively cheesy with anyone else felt perfect with him. Sated, my man stood and motioned for me to follow suit. As he bowed and outstretched his hand for a dance, Akon's "Don't Matter" played (It don't matter/ that nobody wanna see us together). We laughed.

"Can I sleepover tonight?" he asked, eyebrows raised, chin tucked in.

I knew this head orientation. Sasha was reserving his enthusiasm until I reacted according to hunch. "Of course!" I said. There was no other answer when given the option of a full night nestled in his arms. I would do anything to extend any of our encounters.

My next thoughts were unwelcome, though. How would Sasha explain an overnight absence to his wife? Would he shower before encountering her like a devout Catholic intent on wiping the dirt off after sex? Why did this illicit arrangement, which mandated thinking such things, work so well for me? Was I empowered, or weak? Was a dalliance all I could handle in addition to Céline? If she were healthy, would I feel differently?

Desperate to abandon these irritating thoughts, I spasmed like a pest with a snapped neck trying, in vain, to free itself from a trap. At least, I imagined spasming. In reality I let him hold me, and as soon as our eyes met, I felt safe again, bathing in our togetherness.

As the song faded, I turned to the clock. Though I hadn't worn a watch since Wall Street, I kept track of our time vigilantly.

"You have a beautiful profile," Sasha said.

Did I hear him right? My nose was a sensitive subject since I had been asked so many times if I'd broken it in the past. The unsightly bump at its center practically begged the question. But the moment smelled genuine. Céline once told me she was desperate to be loved—for any reason other than her intelligence. I finally understood this sentiment. It's easy to appreciate someone's greatest talents or traits or even their quirks, but when you find someone whose flaws you adore and who, in turn, appreciates yours, it all makes sense.

"Thank you," I said, more grateful than Sasha could know.

***

Startled awake by the doorbell, I sifted through a mental list of possible visitors. I had curbed my online shopping habit long ago, so I wasn't expecting any packages, and I was relatively certain Sasha's wife had no way of tracking down my address. A second ring led me to consult the peephole, which revealed a FedEx deliveryman. In my morning stupor, I allowed myself to indulge the possibility that my sushi article had gone viral overnight and that the man standing before me was a fervent fish rights activist disguised as a FedEx representative. But my daydream was soon shattered by a return address. The man before me held a parcel from the rehab facility my sister had been admitted to less than a fortnight earlier. The arrival of this box at my door told me, in heart-wrenchingly definitive terms, that she had checked out early.

As I dismantled the boomerang care package, the year Céline started at Columbia inevitably came to mind. Saddened to be home without my sister, I mailed her frequent notes that year—some just to say I'd be heading to bed after finishing my homework, dreading the alarm clock buzzer that would wake me in place of her not-so-gentle shoulder poking. Every letter was written on Winnie the Pooh stationery she'd gifted me with for Christmas. In truth, my obsession with that pudgy bear wasn't authentic; it was a reaction to Céline's fixation with Smurfs. I wanted to collect thematic paraphernalia because she did. I sent Céline countless packages containing baked goods that year, too. Baking from scratch had always aligned us because Mom was adamantly opposed to boxed mixes, which she equated with another highly offensive item sold in American grocery stores: Cheez Whiz. On weekend afternoons, Céline and I would don oversized aprons and sift through Mom's recipe books. We made brownies, sugar cookies, lemon squares, shortbread and cakes of all kinds. Though I didn't typically take instruction from her easily, I enjoyed letting my older sister teach me how to shimmy a measuring cup so the flour would level out, how to avoid over mixing, and how to prick something with a fork to see if it was cooked. I played sous chef happily.

By comparison, this package was depressingly serious. It included a bag of Céline's favorite candy, Starbursts, a handwritten letter commending her courage, and James Frey's A

Million Little Pieces, which I'd read in a maybe-lame attempt to understand her.

"Funny how good intentions can cause more heartache than joy," I said.

Sasha comprehended the gravity of the situation without pressing for elaboration. He lingered longer than I knew he could that day, but eventually he had to take off and that was okay. I was lost in my own head anyway.

A few hours later, I received an email from Vanity's Fair Michael Hogan reporting that the traffic from my sushi piece was "off the charts." He wanted to assign me another "immersive" story and asked for ideas.

I had a choice: I could wallow in the murky remnants of a futile care package, or I could reply. Driven by the seedling of an intriguing concept that had surfaced thanks to Sasha, I chose to sit and formulate a pitch. Schnoz aside, I've always felt pretty secure about my looks. And yet, we are all so vulnerable to remarks, negative or positive, about our appearance. I was determined to pursue an undercover plastic surgery story in which I would give three doctors free reign to "make me more beautiful," so I could see how far they would go in encouraging a healthy 20-something to get work done. Hogan green lit the concept immediately and offered me a $1,000 fee, which was twice what I had earned for the sushi piece.

Topped with sorrow, success tasted strange. But no matter what had happened to Céline, I had to live my life. I owed that to her as much as to myself.

V

Behind her professional exterior, nurse Marina truly feels for us. How could she not? Expertly, she maneuvers amongst the tentacles of tubes keeping my sister "alive" to administer more Ativan and cut off the supply of blood pressure meds. Has she done this before? How many times?

Within minutes, Céline's seizures are yet less forgiving. Can she sense our presence? *I love you so much!* I want to shout, but don't.

The four of us barely speak. Even our weeping is relatively silent. Is anguish anger's quieter cousin? At 27, am I supposed to understand the difference?

When a priest arrives to perform the sacrament of Last Rites, I feel surprisingly at ease. Normally, ritualism seems too creepy to tolerate. After years of attending weekly mass, Céline, Damien and I all went in the direction of agnosticism. For now, though, neither Dad's bowed head nor the concept of God irks.

During a particularly lengthy seizure, I squeeze Céline's hand as hard as I can, pleading with the

Universe to spare her pain. Her fingers are the same misshapen ones I have. Dad has. But her flesh is strangely more glutinous. I restrain myself from bending down to hug her as tightly as possible. Why?

Ten minutes pass before the pace of her statistics' plummet quickens. Between sniffles and wipes of dry, cheap tissue across my face, I ponder my sister's brief existence. The triumphs: so many good grades. The failures: not getting into Yale. A girl so bright, talented, and special. *Could you be more clichéd?* I hear Céline grumble. I think of the electronics pawned out of desperation. The friends and colleagues alienated. The criminal cokehead ex-boyfriend she met during an unfinished stint in rehab. The abortion. The lies. The deceits. The mistakes. I see Céline as the lush she was. The brilliant thinker she was. The intellect who wanted to be loved for anything but her brain. The sister, the daughter, the friend. I am different. I am the same.

On April 5th, 2009, at 5:10pm, by every medical measure, my sister is dead.

Awestruck, exhausted, relieved, and sad, I exit her room in the ICU one last time. At once, the void is evident. Nothing matters—and yet, everything does. She is gone. Released from corporeal imprisonment.

Did she want this end?

***

It felt odd to enter Saint Vincent's over the winter of 2009 for any reason other than to visit Céline, but the nearest gathering of Al Anon, the sister organization to Alcoholics Anonymous for the friends and relatives of problem drinkers, was held there.

Apprehensive but purposeful, tired of feeling ashamed and helpless, I took my seat at a long wooden table in a remote wing of the hospital. As I waited for a guy in a wool beanie sitting cross-legged atop the table (hopefully our group leader and not some wandering psych patient) to speak, I looked around. Most people were already clutching tissues and everyone looked desperate to unburden themselves. Can you redistribute misery?

Following Wool Beanie's standard welcome, he invited each of us to share an adjective that best described our current state of mind. Apparently, this was how the session would end too. The assumption that my mood might change in the slightest within the hour annoyed me.

With a wink at our leader that said she was a regular, a black lady in a pencil skirt and blazer piped up. "Reflective," she said. Next, a C-list actor I recognized from several minor television roles leaned forward, elbows resting on knees, to utter "fine." As my turn approached, I tried not to disregard the exercise as silly, but I was less than eager to share my innermost thoughts aloud with strangers. Plus, no single word accurately encapsulated my mindset. I felt angry, confounded, sad, grateful (I was the lucky one who required Al Anon rather than AA, right?), helpless, frustrated, skeptical, etc. Emotionally, I was one undesirably sticky mess. Avoiding eye contact with everyone, I chose "messy."

Next, stranger after stranger volunteered stories about loved ones affected by alcoholism. Each account was equally touching. But what was most striking was that no one else seemed to know an alcoholic as young or in as dire a condition as Céline. Must the girl over-achieve at everything?

I left St. Vincent's yet more confused by the organization that was supposed to help me. Was this how my sister felt about rehab?

The next day, I decided I had no recourse other than to stop speaking to my sister—to make it clear that I couldn't condone her behavior. As I called to alert her, the monotony of ringing hypnotized me into believing that this was absolutely the right course of action. After all, she had refused to listen. And while it was her legal right to ban us from speaking to her doctors, that move seemed unnecessarily harsh.

Toward the end, Céline shared one gem of a medical detail: Her doctors estimated that two percent of her liver, an organ responsible for 2,000 essential bodily functions, was working properly. Unfortunately or not, it's especially difficult for an alcoholic to qualify for a transplant.

In 2008 and 2009, Céline was hospitalized for varying lengths of time on May 11th, July 21st, Sept 16th, Oct 29th, Nov 29th, Dec 26th, March 7th, and April 2nd. In January or February of 2009, I reopened the lines of communication with Céline a few weeks after cutting her off because things looked that grim.

By the spring of 2009, I eulogized my sister nightly before falling asleep.

On April 8, 2009, I deliver the real thing:

Perpetually amused by the world around her, Céline's unique perspective allowed her to opine on Ovid's Metamorphoses and Virgil's Aeneid as fluently and fervently as on Britney Spears' Greatest Hits and movies like Adventures In Babysitting. "An important film," she would say of the latter, and this would make Damien and me laugh—understanding that, although she jested, she also sort of meant it.

Together, the three of us could also always laugh upon mention of the scene in The Lion King when Timon, hypothesizing about how to divert Mufasa's clan of hyenas, asks Simba, "What do you want me to do, dress in drag and do the Hula?" You could sit Céline, Damien and me in front of any movie and we would laugh during all the same moments, however seemingly insignificant, or un-funny. Today I am so grateful for that shared sense of more-than-slightly-off-beat humor (which may or may not be the result of our awesomely odd French parents) that Damien and I can still cherish...

...During the last few years, even as her family, it was difficult to be by Céline's side. Often, admittedly, I was not. But no matter how many days I lost, because, out of anger, I refused to speak to her, I feel at ease.

I feel at ease because I know my sister. I know that she knew she made mistakes, and that her missteps had a hurtful impact on others. I also know that Céline never sought forgiveness, probably because she never felt she deserved it.

Céline didn't aim to make excuses for herself. Her integrity didn't allow for that. My sister was too dignified, too self-aware, and too smart for that...

***

Before guests arrive for the memorial service, I rifle through Céline's old room. Amidst her bras and underwear, I discover a black and white composition notebook containing a sole journal entry. I admire my sister's penmanship, remembering the hours I spent as a kid trying to mimic it even though she was left-handed and I was a righty.

Seated on Céline's old twin bed, I dig in.

Here today I find myself having just been admitted to the psychiatric ward at St. Vincent's hospital in lower Manhattan. The story that has led me to this place is not easily narrated succinctly, nor do I wish to indulge in a tedious rehashing of it at this time. If you're reading this, one of three circumstances must be true:

1. *You are in fact me*
2. *You are a terrible snoop*

Through tears, I laugh, proud to know this is directed at me—at least, proud to be the person she knew so fucking well.

3. *I have died and this trifle of ramblings has surfaced in the cleaning out of my belongings.*

None of these cases inspires me to present a recent, cohesive history about myself for fairly self-evident reasons.

I mention that I may be dead if these words are being read. It is something I ponder lately—my own longevity. I may in fact be on my way out, an idea I have not borne out of some morbid fascination with melodrama, but rather is a fear shared by numerous members of the medical community.

So here I find myself in the psych ward, on the 5th floor, which I'm continuously assured is for the "least crazy" or "most stable" of us, though I'm entirely unconvinced the patients on floors 1-4 don't hear the same chorus. Anyway, I landed myself here "voluntarily," though strongly recommended by the physicians I saw over the course of the past 6 days, which I spent hospitalized across the street for delightful ailments such as vomiting blood, etc.—details neither necessary nor interesting. Bottom line: They didn't want to let me loose on the street because they deemed me to be thoroughly depressed, and, perhaps of more immediate potential liability to them, suicidal.

I probably am depressed—this I concede fully. However, I maintain that I am not now, and never have been, a suicidal person—if only because I'm much too terrified of dying (dying, not death—an important distinction in my way of thinking).

Well, off to bed now. I'm actually feeling properly sleepy, and not just direly fatigued as over the past few months. This would be more satisfying if I could claim it to be indicative of some natural healing process within my body, but I must instead attribute the welcome prospect of impending slumber to a tiny little pill. Apparently they've found one that won't (or shouldn't) do any additional damage to my already fucked up liver. I can only hope I'm not facing eight hours of horrifying nightmares.

Wow, I sound cynical and bitter this evening. I think I'm a relatively pleasant person in reality, so I'll cease today's ramblings before I get on my own nerves.

In the grand tradition of the most illustrious Jerry Springer, a "final thought": "She said she usually cried at least once each day not because she was sad, but because the world was so beautiful and life was so short."

I close the notebook and wipe my cheeks dry, knowing I'll revisit these words again and again and again. In spite of her circumstances, Céline could see beauty. There's no reason why I shouldn't see it everywhere and every day. My sister didn't fear death, and it is my responsibility not to fear life.

***

A few months after the service, my most recent immersive story about Ashley Madison, a website designed to facilitate affairs, goes viral and I option the dramatic rights. I'm officially making a living as a writer, and I know that what I have with Sasha, however socially unacceptable, is unquestionably beautiful.

In choosing my next endeavor, I challenge myself to top my last effort. I don't care what Jesus would do. I ask: What would the girl whose sister inadvertently gifted her with perspective do? The downside of pushing the proverbial envelope is invisible to me, so the answer is pretty much anything. For those who've grown accustomed to shock by necessity, things normalize more quickly, maybe. Whenever embarrassment, shame, fright, or hesitation tickles, I hear my Bird say *I will always love you, Stinky.*

I don't know where I'm going or what I'll do next, but I know who I am. I am a writer, an ardent lover, a dreamer, a daughter, and a friend. And in spite of everything—even death—I am Céline's little sister.

AFTERWORD

50 AWESOME TRUTHS MY SISTER WROTE DOWN BEFORE DYING

Shortly after graduating from high school in 1996, Céline gave each of her friends a handwritten booklet listing some of the things she'd learned by age 18. It was a DIY graduation gift of sorts. As sisters, we shared a lot, but I wasn't aware of this booklet's creation until after Céline died. At the funeral, one of Céline's closest friends kindly supplied me with a copy. Of course it moved me that he'd kept it for so long since I'd like to believe that Céline did a lot of things that had a lasting impact on others.

Mostly, however, reading the booklet made me smile because the decision to distribute something entitled "A Modest Compilation of Truths" at age 18 was so very pretentious—and yet, so very acceptable from a person like my sister, to whom people turned constantly for advice. Part of what made Céline so special is that she could pull this kind of thing off. She could draft something about life truths in adolescence that wouldn't make anyone cringe. Later in adulthood, Céline probably would have cringed at her own "youthful ridiculousness," but knowing that only makes the whole thing even awesomer.

A MODEST COMPILATION OF TRUTHS BY CÉLINE BERLIET

Introduction/Preface/Forward/Whatever:

Well you guys, here it is at last. I guess the graduation present I promised you has turned into more of a going away present. Such is life, I suppose.

Before I continue I would like to apologize for the messiness of this handwritten booklet. I really did intend to type this up for all of you, but as many of you know, computers hate me. In fact, the feeling is mutual. Since I've had a bit of time on my hands here in France, I decided I'd just write up my book and distribute it upon my return.

So anyway, here it is. But before you begin reading my little book, there are a few things I'd like all of you to consider and understand:

- You may have noted that I titled this book a "modest compilation," rather than an "instruction book." This is not my arrogant attempt to teach any of you anything. In fact, much of the book reflects things that you have taught me, or that I have somehow learned in my daily dealings with all of you.

- You may also have noted the word "truth" in the title of this book. That is because, as many of you know, I am a big believer in and fan of truth. I believe that every statement within this book contains at least a particle of truth. Of course, you may very well disagree with me. I am certainly not the all-knowing seer of truths. However, every statement contained in this book has, I believe, opened my eyes a bit wider, or somehow rounded out my still not-so-round vision of truth.

- You will notice as you flip through these pages that a good portion of this book is quotes, rather than my own personal thoughts. Well, as I said before, I search mainly for truth. How arrogant it would be of me to look only within myself for something so great!

- Remember that just because your name isn't cited as the source of any statement in this book, it doesn't mean you haven't contributed to its development. All of you have, in fact, shown me truths at one time or another, and that is why I value and love you guys so much.

Enjoy. This is the one thing, out of the 103 I was supposed to do, that I actually did...

1. A conversation between Calvin and Hobbes:

Calvin: They say the world is a stage. But obviously the play is unrehearsed and everybody is adlibbing his lines.

Hobbes: Maybe that's why it's hard to tell if we're in a tragedy or a farce?

Calvin: We need more special effects and dance numbers.

2. "Every gambler knows the secret to surviving is knowing what to throw away and knowing what to keep." – The Gambler, Kenny Rogers

3. "If you are truly confident about something, you welcome honest questions about it." – Peter Kreeft

4. Don't ask people questions you know they can't answer.

5. Search less for meaning and more for truth.

6. Yes, quite often it is the case that bad people get good parking spots. Don't waste your time being bitter about it.

7. Verb a word.

8. "Blessed is the man, who having nothing to say, abstains from giving wordy evidence of the fact." – George Eliot

9. "The difference between a fool and a jerk is that a fool does stupid things that only hurt himself, whereas a jerk does stupid things that hurt others." – Dave Harvey

10. Security often comes from knowing yourself better than other people know you.

11. Most truths are intuitively obvious and remarkably simple.
12. He who knows not and knows not that he knows not is a fool; shun him. He who knows not and knows that he knows not is a child; teach him. He who knows and knows not that he knows is asleep; wake him. He who knows and knows that he knows is wise; follow him. (An old saying from I forget which country)
13. "People rarely change, but all too often become "more so" of a quality they always possessed but never expressed." – Mr. McKeon
14. Beware of people who insist on telling others how much of a rock star they are.
15. Understand the difference between procrastinating and taking time out to relax.
16. "Don't be so open-minded that your brains falls out." (I forgot who said that)
17. "There are those men who say to repay evil with kindness. But I say, how then are we to repay kindness? Repay kindness with kindness, but repay evil with justice." – Confucius
18. "Those who are awake live in a constant state of amazement." – Buddha (I think)
19. "Practice moderation in moderation." – Buddha (I think)
20. "We cross our bridges when we come to them and burn them behind us, with nothing left to show for our progress

except a memory of the smell of smoke, and a presumption that once our eyes watered." – Tom Stoppard

21. Beware of the person who has nothing to lose.

22. "War costs money." – Bob Gardner

23. "And this lies in the nature of things: What people are potentially is revealed in actuality by what they produce." – Aristotle

24. The Skin Horse, from the Velveteen Rabbit, on real: "Real isn't how you are made, it's a thing that happens to you. When a child loves you for a long, long time, not just to play with, but really loves you, then you become real...when you are real you don't mind being hurt...it doesn't often happen to people who break easily or have sharp edges..."

25. Abraham Lincoln once said to a man, "Supposing we called a sheep's tail a leg. Then how many legs would the sheep have?" "Why, five of course," the man replied. "No," corrected Abe, "for calling a tail a leg doesn't make it one."

26. The only honest reason to ever believe anything is because it is true—not because it is pleasant, convenient, or will boost your ego.

27. "What's up is not down and if you can't figure that out, we're all fucked." – Smith Vaughan

28. As the "college process" told us, while it is true that good things come in small packages, good news often comes in large envelopes.
29. Honesty is love of truth.
30. "Your values are defined by what you spend your time and money on." – Dave Harvey
31. "I haven't a particle of confidence in a man who has no redeeming petty vices."– Mark Twain
32. "And how does a man benefit if he gains the whole world and loses his soul in the process? For is anything worth more than his soul?" Mark 8:36-7
33. Don't lecture someone after they've already apologized.
34. "Yard by yard, life is hard. Inch by inch, life's a cinch."
35. As a courtesy to those who wish to check the time, press "clear" on the microwave after stopping it in mid-action.
36. To make a mistake and then not correct it is to make another mistake.
37. "Yes, sometimes life leaves us between a rock and a hard place. But flowers grow in between them, and they are beautiful." – Anthony Johnson
38. Anybody who keeps the ability to see beauty never grows old.
39. Sacrifice honesty before integrity. (That's a tough one. Give it some thought before objecting)

40. "It is easy to find fault, if one has that disposition. There once was a man, who not being able to find any other fault with his coal, complained that there were too many prehistoric toads in it." – Mark Twain

41. Mean people suck.

42. "We are all in the same boat, in a stormy sea, and we owe each other a terrible loyalty." – G.K. Chesterton

43. "Courage is resistance to fear, mastery of fear—not absence of fear." – Mark Twain

44. Most people may in fact be boring or disappointing, but this doesn't make them worthless.

45. The opposite of love is not hate, but indifference.

46. "Pleasant is only the activity of the present, the hope of the future, and the memory of the past."

47. "A Cold, self-righteous prig who goes to church regularly may be far nearer to hell than a prostitute. But, of course, it is better to be neither." – C.S. Lewis

48. "Friends enhance our ability to think and act." – Aristotle

49. "Life moves pretty fast. If you don't stop to look around once in a while, you could miss it." – Ferris Bueller

50. "And she said she usually cried at least once each day, not because she was sad, but because the world was so beautiful and life was so short." – Brian Andreas

A MEDIUM CONTACTED ME WITH A MESSAGE FROM MY DEAD SISTER

A few weeks after publishing the ebook edition of *Surviving In Spirit*, I received the following message via Facebook:

> Hey! This may be the weirdest email you get today and I'm sorry. But I'm pretty sure your sister is trying to get a message to you. I'm not a psychic but I have the ability in some capacity. My mom is able to talk to the other side and I just conferred with her. I was trying not to say anything but sometimes it's impossible. Here's my cell if you feel like talking...

As a non-religious person skeptical of anything otherworldly, I've never consulted a psychic, nor taken my horoscope seriously. On the rare occasion a friend insists on reading Astrology Zone aloud to me (I'm a Leo), I end up twitching between over-excitement ("You are capable of making quite a bit of money this month!") and utter befuddlement ("An unusually sweet new moon...will energize your eighth house") before resigning myself to the fact that a vague predictive outline is just that—even where seemingly accurate. Isn't it senseless to group humans' destinies into one of twelve blurry forecasts dependent upon the calendar day on which they're born? Isn't it yet more senseless to pay a stranger to supply impossible-to-verify hints about what the future may or may not hold?

All of that said, how could I not call the lady claiming to be in touch with my deceased older sister?

Equipped with a pen and paper—for doodling in case of boredom, or for the writing down of mind-boggling revelations, I wasn't quite sure—I dialed the alleged medium's number. No one answered, which was both unexpected and unexpectedly frustrating. How long does a gal have to wait for a line to the other side?

Apparently, about an hour.

When my phone finally rang, I braced myself to be under- or over- whelmed.

At first, I was mostly struck by how easily our conversation flowed—as if we were close friends catching up after a lengthy absence. It turns out that we both had Lyme disease as young adults, and worked in finance right out of college. Were these similarities somehow to account for the medium's as yet revealed insights?

Eager to get down to business, I said, "So you're in contact with Céline?"

The medium explained that the second after she finished reading *Surviving In Spirit*, her phone vibrated off the table. Though comforted by her willingness to admit that she had read my work, I doubted that a vibrating phone could qualify as mystical symbolism. Nevertheless, I encouraged her to go on.

"I had the distinct feeling that your sister was present," she said. "Then, the next morning, my husband came back from the garage to ask why all of his car windows and the sun roof were wide open in 20-degree weather."

"You think my sister did that?"

"Yes. And since I didn't really want your sister's spirit lingering in the house, I knew I had to consult my mom, who's an experienced medium, whereas I'm less comfortable with my connection."

"I see," I said, officially intrigued.

After providing her mom with a few details about me and the book I had written, my amateur psychic friend got the full report: "Céline is really happy and she wants you guys to know that she's at peace. She was a stranger here on Earth and that feeling of being a stranger was too much for her to bear. Her only sadness now is that she's sorry for what she put you guys through, especially your mom."

These statements, however recognizably hazy, triggered tears. It didn't matter that nothing impressively insightful had been said. I was crying—and it felt good, mostly.

She continued, "There was a man in her life whose names starts with a *d*. A lover, maybe? David?"

"Damien," I sniffled. "Our little brother."

"She wants to say that she's really sorry to him for everything too—for what she put him through."

By this point I wept, because it made so much sense that Céline would specifically mention my mom and brother. While Dad and I have proactively pursued measures to cope with Céline's death—he through religion and therapy, me through writing—it would be fair to say that my brother and mother have struggled more.

"There's lots of music around her. It's orchestral!" the medium added.

"She adored music," I confirmed, barely caring that I'd mentioned my sister's musical prowess in *Surviving In Spirit*.

"Céline was beyond this life," the medium said, her tone dauntingly soothing. "Your sister's brilliance was too much even for the people who loved her. She couldn't help herself. It was in no way at all your family's fault."

Emotionally exhausted, but also relieved, I asked whether there was anything else I should know.

As if directly addressing my inner skeptic, the amateur medium assured me that she had tested her mother by asking her about Céline's appearance. (She herself had seen the photographs of Céline and me in my ebook.) Reportedly, mama medium knew that Céline had shoulder length brown hair, and that, "she didn't wear makeup, and never cared."

"Thank you," I said. "This has been wonderful."

Since that phone call, I can't claim an official spiritual conversion. I doubt I will ever pay money to speak to a psychic or a medium (the one who contacted me did so out of kindness, free of charge), and I don't plan to start reading my horoscope regularly. But if a tarot card reader is stationed at an event I attend, as in the case of a recent bridal shower, I will jump at the opportunity to sit with them.

Lately, I am also more open to *signs*—fully aware that once you start looking, you are bound to find them: in the mysterious dark brown hair clinging to the washing machine; in the toothless, bald panhandler's choice to sing ABBA's "Dancing Queen," one of Céline's all-time favorites; and in the odd way a street lamp is reflected on a building's glass façade so that two "walk" figures are visible, one looming above the other, as if protecting her forever. Each of these discrete, meaningful or silly symbols has left me smiling.

In the end, I didn't need the medium's words to be unequivocally true. Or proof that she had interacted with my sister. What I needed, without knowing it, was the sense that Céline's energy—her spirit, I suppose—might still be circulating this world.

ABOUT THE WRITER

Mélanie Berliet is a writer and producer who specializes in going undercover to infiltrate fascinating subcultures so she can report on her insider experiences. The immersive journalist's work has appeared in *Vanity Fair, Elle, Cosmopolitan, New York Magazine, The Atlantic, Pacific Standard, The New York Observer, Esquire, Playboy*, Thought Catalog, and other major publications. Many of Berliet's stories have gone viral, and she is frequently invited to discuss her work and her unique investigative approach on national television. As a producer, Berliet consulted on MTV's hit unscripted show, *The Buried Life*. She also creates original programming for both the web and television.

WHY I'M NAKED ON THE COVER

While brainstorming artwork options for *Surviving In Spirit's* cover, it hit me that posing in the buff was the only way to express the sense of vulnerability that overpowered me the second my 30-year-old sister died. To this day, "naked" is the one word that sums up the very specific way I feel—lonely, helpless, sad, small, accepting, relieved, perplexed, grateful, and so very human all at once—whenever I think about Céline. Nudity is raw, untouched, and defenseless. It is also beautiful. Intent on conveying my deepest, sincerest emotions, I enlisted the world-renowned Michel Tcherevoff (who happens to be my boyfriend's father), to photograph me stripped of clothing and any pretense. Thanks to Michel, this book's cover turned out exactly as awesome as I'd hoped.